LATE NIGHT THOUGHTS

Demi Ruth Queddeng

BookLeaf Publishing
India | USA | UK

Presentation by *BookLeaf Publishing*

Web: www.bookleafpub.com

E-mail: info@bookleafpub.com

ISBN: 9789357447409

First edition 2022

DEDICATION

I wish to show my appreciation by dedicating this to them to take this opportunity to challenge myself and be better.

ACKNOWLEDGEMENT

I am incredibly grateful to the people I have spent my time with because, without them, I would not be able to grasp the meaning of living, love, and choosing what I think is suitable for me.

Thank you for your unconditional support to my family, especially my mom, who taught me countless things.

To the friends who stayed with me even in the distance, DE POTATOS, Thank you.

To the friends who gave me nicknames and established friendships with me, Thank you.

And to the people who left, showed a toxic attitude towards me, I commend myself for cutting them out in my life. I genuinely hope that we will both heal from the hurtful experiences we had in the past.

Lastly, I commend myself for growth over the years and for choosing always to make love prevail and never to hold a grudge against the people who have wronged me.

I highly appreciate you.

PREFACE

Having a walk through the neighborhood, jamming in dad's car with your not kind of music, and just staring at a blank space has made me think about a lot of random things constantly pushing me and ending up with writing poems and short journals about what happened to my day and how was it. What has always been scary to me is overthinking, which I am putting effort into working on. I write them down and keep a journal and a pen beside my bed, old-style, I know, but sometimes I take my phone and type the ideas that go out in my head whenever thoughts just come out right then and there, anywhere. I wanted to share these pieces that I have worked on and will be working on during this period. I want to express myself and share these, and hopefully, we can all relate to each other.

In love with the ocean

Two hearts in a plain space,
Loud drums were drifting like sea waves.
Two people on the ocean floor,
Music beating loud,
Their senses ask for more.

A walk in the scarlet night

Still, she asks for dark curtains.
Moons hide when she walks during the night.
With her crimson dress and burgundy eyes,
Everything turns blank.

Eyes red closed

Dark curtains on the peeking light,
Still red when I close my eyes.
Dwelling in this persistent grey world,
With a poisoned footing and a blank canvas.

A teary twilight

Silhouettes in my dream hug each other,
Tears were leaving my eyes as I awake.
I was dreaming.
Now, even hearing the word "sleep" makes me
shudder.
I am afraid.

Alibi

Up the blue skies,
She got green eyes.
He is a serpent,
Full of lies.

Certitude

Risks stay up in the clouds,
If you want to fly,
Build your wings and go high,
And even if you would not be so sure,
And even if the sky will always stay blue,
The biggest star will forever wait for you.

You're a significant flex

He is a significant flex,
His smile alone gives you to therapy,
His voice makes you tingle hastily,
He can communicate with no demands,
Hugs you with no price,
Treats you like a queen,
No binds,
No lies,
Just loving you with all his might.
He is my fan,
He is my man,
He is a significant flex.

A weekends rest

The weekends sets my heart on fire,
These moments give me peace,
Please do not put down the lyre.

I am but a helpless animal

Yet again,
Today, I felt nothing.

Though as if when I look at these mementoes,
I feel so numb.

His kiss on my left cheek,
As if it's faded.

The message I once felt so in love,
As if it's neglected.

Though as if my soul is syringed with
anaesthesia,
But felt aye, day and night,
Endless.

If these memories persist,
As if my wit is at its end.

Today I told my friends that I would sleep,

As if I always felt weary.

Tonight I sleep with a lonely heart,
As if it's on its way to the anonymous.

And though my stomach wants to cry,
My eyes would not want to budge.

Lightheaded as these 'trusts' pressure me,
As I over reckon,
It is gradually knocking me.

Down to the Earth,
Where animals, like I am, are meant to be.

This day started that I realized,
It takes one life,
To help me.

It takes me.

Me.

Judas Kiss

Even pretty girls get hoaxed,
She is a love giver,
Still, some guys try to play her.
She got no time to play petty games,
Even in betrayal,
She chooses that love prevails.

Letting it go

Meet you one last time,
Back to the very first time,
And entirely walk past you.
And will not ever choose to,
See you in the soil.

Sweet sunset

The moment I decide to look at you,
You always hide,
Either behind a utility pole,
Either behind leaves of a tree,
Either behind the clouds,
And yet,
You're most beautiful when you do that,
Even behind the horizon.

In my next life

It only took one look,

It only took a second to speak,

There's something more than just saying it,

But it always felt like distance is against it,

It's 2:10 in the am,

Still thinking of you this weekend,

But babe, in the end, we die,

In the next lifetime,

I will still always try.

Because in this life,

I finally found the time,

To make it right with you,

And even though these scars have not yet
healed,

I still will choose,

To love you.

Lives don't last too long,

But I'll cherish this moment,

It wouldn't be wrong,

Because babe, this is my last chance,

Choose me now, and I would

not just say it once.

I love you,

Forever,

More than infinity times.

She, Her, My Monica

She's my only euphoria,
A genuine keeper.

She's my beautiful song amidst a ferocious
storm,
My melomaniac.

She makes time worth spending.
And if you ask humbly,
She would gladly share it in her own volition.

Her voice heals my untold wounds that medicine
can't.
She is my great comfort.
My home of relief.

My Monica,
So ever fragile and forgiving.
The bedrock of my heart,
And the frame of my mind.

Meant to be

I'll ask the wind to lead me to you.
Pray to the sky to keep me with you.
Hope to the Earth to let me walk with you.

Wherefore the future will always speak hello to
the sun.
My lover, My darling, My partner in
death-defying quests,
No matter what, hold on because when you do,
these roots tell me that you will always be the
one, my one.

And forever would not be just a word.
So did the oceans blessed me infinity.
So did the trees witnessed our ghosts.
So did the flowers and animals danced with
what we were always bound to have.

That even in the renascence, nature sided with
you, with me, with us.

And so did they attend our ever-crossing reality.
What we have will have and always will be
authentic.

My my playboy

This man always got the time,
He always had wings that no one could see,
A masterpiece of escapades and jollity.

He keeps his word all the same challenges your
heart,
"Respect" reflects on his name,
If you laugh, it is him you should blame.

This text is leading to nowhere,
However, when we held hands,
He always displayed how happy it is to be alive.

And though my damsel you feel this way,
Do remember that,
I am but a playboy.

No matter what

If I have always been a part of your writings,
I'd still want to meet you on your following
books.
With the presumably boundless human
evolution,
Love grows more than a mountain of
connotations,
So does life begin a legion of chapters?
And all these things end with a single blink.
but baby, through all these things,
I would still like to see it, fight it, and work it
through with you.
Because even after death, I know,
I would still want you to be mine.
I love you,
And if forever is a chance,
I'll make it through and through,
And I will always choose you.

His name is Aries

Your name is beautiful,
It sounded like stars.
You remind me of the beauty of the galaxy,
Both bright and dark.

Your name is beautiful,
I imagine the stars reflect from your eyes.
So is your eyes,
I imagine them looking at me with a sweet gaze.

And though we are but far from each other,
We will both hope that soon,
We touch one another.

Be your home, Be my home

And if you were to find me in this chaos,
Hug me and tell me that you need me.
And if you ever doubt it,
Just always think that we are meant to be.
Because in my world,
We both belong.

She is a classic

She is a classic,
Falling for her is automatic.
She makes me feel like levitating,
Each of her smiles is cunning.

You make me feel like levitating.

I wrote you a poem,
And now it is stuck in my head.

I wonder about time,
            distance,
        and velocity.
And how the universe is full of these so-called
spectra.
I levitate.

www.ingramcontent.com/pod-product-compliance
Lightning Source LLC
LaVergne TN
LVHW021341200726
843509LV00014B/2619

9 789357 447409